Original title:
Whispers Beneath the Leaves

Copyright © 2025 Creative Arts Management OÜ
All rights reserved.

Author: Elias Marchant
ISBN HARDBACK: 978-1-80567-076-6
ISBN PAPERBACK: 978-1-80567-156-5

The Enigma of Twilight Leaves

In the grove where shadows play,
A squirrel tangled in ballet,
Dancing to the tune of night,
Tail a-feather, quite a sight!

The owl hoots with a cheeky grin,
As crickets join the din within,
With mischief in their chirpy ways,
They turn the dusk to bright buffets!

A breeze sifts through the jesting trees,
Tickling branches like a tease,
Twirling leaves, a grand parade,
Marching forth in leafy braid.

The moon peeks in, a watchful eye,
Counting every leaf that flies,
A giggle erupts, the night's alive,
Where nature's jokes will always thrive!

The Sweetness of Silent Conversations

Under the boughs, secrets float,
Squirrels gossip, chipping like a boat.
The breeze pulls jokes from tall trunks,
While the shadows dance, stirring their clunks.

A frog croaks, as the sun gives a grin,
Tree ants march like they're in a spin.
Laughter bubbles from sapling roots,
While wise old owls wear their best suits.

Harboring Hidden Thoughts

In the canopy, a secret chat,
A raccoon grins while wearing a hat.
The branches creak with teasing sound,
While fireflies waltz, circling around.

Leaves hide giggles from wandering feet,
As tiny blooms gather, sharing a treat.
Acorns chuckle in their cozy shells,
Telling tales that the wise tree tells.

Echoing the Fables of the Forest

Fables flop from thick mossy beds,
As chipmunks weave tales with tiny threads.
The mighty oak stands, listening near,
While playful winds carry all that cheer.

Beneath the canopy, the stories twine,
Mushrooms giggle over sips of brine.
The breeze whispers jokes to the tallest pine,
As shadows hide laughter, oh so divine.

The Tapestry of Tree Tales

Every branch strums a silly tune,
As critters dance beneath the moon.
The bark of trees seems to crack a smile,
While playful winds pause for a while.

Furry friends gather for a prank,
On a soft log by the riverbank.
The canopy hums with mischievous glee,
As nature tells tales, oh so carefree.

The Gentle Breath of Green Companions

In trees so tall, they play hide and seek,
With branches that tickle, they giggle and squeak.
The squirrels in court jest with clever design,
While owls roll their eyes at their antics divine.

The grass sways in rhythm, a comical dance,
As dandelion seeds drift, taking their chance.
The mushrooms are jesters, with caps oh so bright,
While snails in tuxedos are quite the sight!

Riddles Carved in Shadows

In shadowy corners where laughter does dwell,
The moon plays a tune, a humor to tell.
A raccoon in shorts tries to scale a tall fence,
The audience gasps, will he jump - suspense!

Among ancient trees, secrets tickle the air,
Entwined with the breeze, a whimsical flair.
The toads in their bow ties recite jokes from afar,
While fireflies giggle, blushing like stars.

The Ballad of the Darkened Grove

In a darkened grove where the shadows play tricks,
The crickets make puns, their chirps like quick flicks.
A hedgehog on roller skates dodges a chase,
While rabbits debate who has the best face.

The moon snorts with laughter, the night laughs along,
As the trees rustle softly, sharing their song.
Each rustle a chuckle, each breeze a delight,
In this grove of giggles, beneath starlit night.

Memories of Mossy Grottos

In mossy niches where chuckles reside,
The gnomes tell tall tales, with a wink and a slide.
A beetle with glasses reads jokes from a shell,
While bushes all blush, sharing secrets they tell.

The fungi form circles for laughter anew,
Trading silly stories as old as the dew.
With laughter contagious, the shadows entwine,
In grottos of giggles, where mischief does shine.

Veils of Verdant Mystery

In the forest where squirrels play,
A pinecone fell in a funny way.
The trees chuckled, they knew the chat,
Of critters plotting a sneaky spat.

Sassafras claimed the best hiding spot,
But every acorn gave away the plot.
The bushes shook with laughter near,
As chipmunks danced without a fear.

The Cadence of Bark and Leaf

Beneath the shade, a rabbit pranced,
Chasing shadows, it almost danced!
A wise old owl hooted with glee,
As the leaves joined in a silly spree.

A twig snapped loud, made everyone pause,
The hedgehog giggled, 'What's the cause?'
For every rustle, there's a good tale,
Of forest fun that will surely prevail.

Unraveled Serenades of Nature

The brook began to hum a tune,
While frogs croaked under the light of the moon.
They formed a band, a merry crew,
With a turtle tapping its feet, oh, so true.

Dancing daisies in a gentle breeze,
Tickle-sticks swaying, as if to tease.
Nature's laughter rang through the hollow,
As butterflies twirled, no one could follow.

The Stories of the Stillness

In the quiet, a snail told its tale,
Of wandering freely without a trail.
It's slow and steady, said with a grin,
In the race of life, who cares to win?

A ladybug blurted, "I'm on a quest,"
While ants marched forward, never at rest.
The stories here are sweet and quirky,
Of garden capers that are truly jerky.

Soft Serenades of the Wilderness

In the woods where critters sing,
A squirrel plays the tambourine.
The owl hoots, a comical note,
As the rabbit dances, donning a coat.

The raccoon croons in a silly way,
While the frogs join in, a cabaret.
A wise old turtle rolls his eyes,
As the fox tells jokes beneath the skies.

The breeze carries laughter, sweet and light,
As chipmunks chatter, a boisterous sight.
Oh, what a ruckus, what a riot,
In the wild, where giggles never die, it.

So let's gather 'round, share a laugh or two,
The forest's humor shines bright and true.
In this merry realm, all worries cease,
Nature's fun is a joyous feast!

Hushed Conversations in the Grove

In the grove where shadows play,
A gnome loses his hat today.
The owls roll eyes, they snicker low,
As the hedgehog joins in the show.

The bushes rustle with gossip rare,
A tortoise scolds a hare with flair.
Each tree has tales, both silly and bold,
Of acorns lost and mushrooms sold.

Chattering sparrows line the tall fence,
Debating the merits of their defense.
The mice in their outfits squeak and chime,
"Did you see that tumble? Oh, what a crime!"

So listen close, as nature unfolds,
A comedy waiting, a story told.
In the grove of mirth where laughter weaves,
Play along, all are welcome, believe!

Voices of the Rustling Boughs

In boughs that sway with playful glee,
A parrot jokes, "Hey, look at me!"
The branches giggle, they sway and sway,
As the sun shares stories of a brighter day.

A crow caws loudly, a rascal in fact,
Stealing snacks, he shows no tact.
The woodpecker drums, keeping the beat,
As the leaves shuffle, moving their feet.

The wind jests softly, tickling the trees,
"Oh, don't you dare!" they rustle with ease.
A picnic of laughter, let's not ignore,
Nature's own jesters, forever encore.

With critters gossiping and laughter abound,
In this lively theater, joy can be found.
So raise a toast to the jests in the sun,
In this humorous realm, life's even more fun!

The Secrets Held by the Trees

In a glade where giggles hide,
Trees tell secrets with pride.
The acorns sigh, "Oh, what a fuss!"
As the wind giggles, riding the bus.

A bear tells tales, not shy at all,
Of honey pots and a wobbly fall.
The fox plays tricks, unaware of the clock,
As the butterflies flutter, laughing in flock.

The shadows chuckle, a mischievous lore,
As the dandelions dance, begging for more.
Each rustling leaf holds a joke untold,
Whimsical whispers that never grow old.

So let's find delight in nature's embrace,
With laughter and stories, we'll quicken our pace.
For in these woods, joy surely we'll see,
In the secrets held by each giddy tree!

Hushed Stories of the Glade

In the forest, critters chatter,
Pine cones tumble, making clatter.
Squirrels gossip, plotting pranks,
While rabbits roll in leafy ranks.

Mice try to steal acorns on the sly,
Bamboozling birds as they fly by.
Frogs croak jokes, the sun keeps score,
Nature's jesters—never a bore!

Nature's Gentle Confessions

Tree trunks giggle at silly ferns,
As bunnies bounce with cheeky turns.
Chirping crickets share their schemes,
Plotting adventure in daytime dreams.

Bees buzz secrets in wild delight,
Stealing nectar, oh what a sight!
The wind carries tales far and wide,
In this leafy play, they take pride.

The Secret Life of Woodland Shadows

Shadows dance, but don't get caught,
Worms are wiggling—what a thought!
Owls practice their best hoots all night,
While raccoons rehearse their heist with fright.

Beneath the moon, a fox cracks jokes,
Tree branches creak like playful folks.
Underneath every shady nook,
There's a giggle, just take a look!

Beneath the Bark's Resonance

Bark giggles as squirrels dig,
Fungi find it all quite big.
Ants march like they own the floor,
With tiny crowns they all adore.

Every rustle tells a tale,
Winds carry laughter down the trail.
Leaves chuckle in the golden sun,
In this kingdom, all have fun!

Leafy Layers of Lore

In the forest's tangled maze,
Squirrels share their nutty tales,
With acorns bouncing here and there,
While gossiping on the trails.

Frogs croak secrets, no one hears,
They leap around in silly play,
Hopping for joy, void of fears,
They make the bushes sway and sway.

Rabbits plot their carrot schemes,
While owls hoot tips for late-night snacks,
Underneath the treetops' beams,
Nature's gatherings have no lacks.

Shadows dance with silly prance,
While rustling leaves burst out in laughter,
Nature's jovial, merry romance,
Is the tale of joy thereafter.

The Dance of Secrets in Green

Lively breezes' tickle tunes,
Trees shake hands in shared delight,
Grasshoppers bring the funny boons,
Each leap is a quirky sight.

Chipmunks wear their acorn hats,
Prancing round like little clowns,
As nature giggles, how it chats,
We all fall down in laughter sounds.

A dance of ferns, a playful sway,
With petals sharing giggly glee,
The wise old trees have much to say,
In circles where joy's so free.

Beneath the boughs, where chuckles reign,
Songs of mirth fill up the air,
Nature's comedy, no refrain,
It's a show beyond compare.

Revelations from the Tree Tops

High above in leafy chairs,
Birds squawk stories full of cheer,
Tails flicker, as if with flair,
They sing of antics far and near.

The shyest leaf makes a bold claim,
Of the best spots for sunshine flair,
While the daisies fuel the game,
With giggles swaying here and there.

The sunbeams join in with a grin,
Tickling toes of ferns and blooms,
Every smile hidden within,
As nature's laughter brightly looms.

From the tallest trees to the ground,
Each creature has a tale to weave,
Altogether, the joy is found,
In the stories that we believe.

Glistening Greetings of the Glade

Morning dew like sparkly cheer,
Kisses petals with a wink,
While crickets chirp a song sincere,
As butterflies begin to think.

Frolic and play through sunshine's gleam,
Each shadow hides a chortled joke,
Laughter swirls in nature's dream,
Among the oaks where spirits poke.

Mossy carpets hold the jest,
As beetles race in silly haste,
A gathering nature loves best,
In fun-filled moments never waste.

Each leap of joy and twitch of leaf,
Brings smiles and giggles all around,
Where friendship grows beyond belief,
In the glade where laughter sounds.

The Silence That Breathes

In the garden, a squirrel sneezes,
Leaves tremble like giggling breezes.
A crow cackles, missing its cue,
While ants march in a busy queue.

A snail performs a sluggish dance,
While flowers play a game of chance.
Butterflies flutter, laughing with glee,
A bumblebee buzzes, sipping his tea.

The shadows shift, they share a chuckle,
As the wind plays an impromptu huddle.
Nature's humor, oh, so absurd,
Where laughter lingers without a word.

Colors clash, a sight so divine,
As daisies gossip, spreading the wine.
In this realm where laughter thrives,
Every rustle keeps our joy alive.

Unseen Voices of the Underbrush

The toads croak jokes by the old oak,
While mushrooms giggle, sharing a poke.
Crickets chirp with rhythmic flair,
As the fox laughs, without a care.

A chipmunk plays a trick on the hare,
With acorns flying through the air.
Each plant dances, regales its tale,
And the frogs join in, ready to sail.

The moon peeks in, a wise, bright sage,
Critters peek out from their leafy page.
The world below has a comic streak,
With every rustle, silly events peak.

Floating dreams on a breeze so light,
The earth chuckles beneath the night.
In shadows deep, laughter's alight,
In the underbrush, pure delight.

The Poetry of Swaying Limbs

Branches wave as if to tease,
Roots entwined in a gentle breeze.
A leaf shimmies, strikes a pose,
While the trunk proudly tells its woes.

A happy twig begins to sing,
To the rhythm of the spring.
Buds nod along to nature's rhyme,
In the woods, it's party time!

The wind enchants with playful tunes,
Shaking shadows beneath the moons.
Dancing daisies all around,
Nature's ballet, laughs abound.

As sunlight winks, the branches sway,
In this theatre, all are gay.
Leaves in laughter, soaked in cheer,
Nature's comedy, crystal clear.

Silent Echoes of Nature's Heart

In a brook, a fish does leap,
With splashy quirks that will not sleep.
Rabbits giggle as they hop,
Their playful leaps, they never stop.

Stones sit grinning on the shore,
As dragonflies spin tales galore.
Crickets play their fiddling strings,
While the breeze struts in, and sings.

An owl smirks from its high abode,
While moths around the lantern goad.
Nighttime mumbles funny dreams,
As laughter drifts through moonlit beams.

Each rustle holds a quirky jest,
In nature's realm, we are all guests.
In this silent chatter, we partake,
A joyful world that wakes, then shakes.

Echoes in the Twilight Green

In the woods where squirrels chatter,
A raccoon sings while munching on batter.
The owls hoot jokes in a serious tone,
Even the trees laugh at the antics shown.

Beneath a bush, a rabbit does a jig,
With carrots in hand, he hops like a big.
The breeze carries giggles, light and spry,
As fireflies blink, saying, 'Oh my, oh my!'

Frogs join in with a croaking refrain,
Dance near the pond like it's all in vain.
The moon tries to keep a straight, calm face,
As the night reveals this curious place.

So let's join the fun, don't miss a beat,
In this twilight green, let's move our feet!
Laughter and joy in the air reside,
Every creature here serves as a guide.

The Soundtrack of Summer's Silence

When the sun takes a nap and the critters play,
A toaster pops toast while bees wiggle and sway.
Grasshoppers strum on their tiny guitars,
And a turtle's slow shuffle beats all the cars.

Chirping crickets run the nightly band,
While a mushroom grows tall, offering its hand.
The ducks quack puns as they waddle and glide,
Every sound is a giggle in nature's wild ride.

Random breezes send ticks and tocks,
Crackling branches sing with giggling knocks.
Each star twinkles back with a wink and a laugh,
It's a silent symphony, a merry gaff.

Listen closely, let joy be your guide,
For in the quiet, the fun will abide.
So grab a chair, take a seat if you dare,
Join this raucous concert found everywhere.

Conversations in the Dappled Light

In a sun-drenched glade, the shadows collide,
A squirrel debates with a dragonfly wide.
'You've got wings, but I've got the nuts!'
They argue and squabble with silly results.

Nearby, a hedgehog tells tales so bold,
While ladybugs giggle at stories retold.
A fox rolls its eyes, says, 'I'm far too cool!'
And slinks through the grass like an old-fashioned fool.

A curious chipmunk hops in to say,
'Your yarns are nice, but I've got to play!'
With a flick of its tail, the party ignites,
As laughter erupts in those dappled sights.

The sun peeks in, joining their spree,
In this giggling world, so wild and free.
Let's share a joke or two, don't be shy,
In these friendly chats, there's no reason to cry.

Murmured Dreams Among the Roots

Unearthed secrets in a playful dance,
Rabbits play poker; we didn't stand a chance!
Badgers laugh, betting hay on their paws,
While a snail reads fortunes with fading applause.

The trees shake their leaves like a grand applause,
While worms tell tales that have no flaws.
With each earthy chuckle, the roots intertwine,
Creating a world where humor will shine.

A wise old owl gives advice with a grin,
'Life of a root is a game to win!'
A beetle clinks glasses with dew drops so fine,
In this underground gala, oh, how they shine!

So dig down below and join the feud,
In dreams full of laughter, let your heart be renewed.
For beneath our feet lies a treasure so bright,
With glimmers of joy in each darkened night.

Nature's Lullaby in Green

In the grove where squirrels play,
The acorns drop in a clumsy way.
They roll and tumble, what a sight!
The critters giggle, oh what a night!

The frogs sing bass, a croaky tune,
While fireflies dance under the moon.
A raccoon steals snacks, what a fun spree!
Nature's party, just you and me!

A woodpecker's drum echoes loud and clear,
While rabbits hop around with no fear.
The grasshoppers join in, a wild brigade,
In this verdant ball, no need to be afraid!

So let's join the fun in this leafy space,
Where trees have laughter written on their face.
With nature's cheer, we'll sway and spin,
In this green lullaby, let the joy begin!

Ghosts of the Whispering Wood

In the eerie grove, where shadows creep,
The ghosts lost their way, they're half asleep.
They trip on roots and sigh with dread,
'Not again!' they moan, 'We just ate bread!'

One ghost sneezes, a booming sound,
Boo! The deer jump up from the ground.
'Haunting's hard when you can't float,'
They chuckle softly, sharing a coat.

A jolly specter with a silly grin,
Waves to a passing owl, 'Let the fun begin!'
With dancing leaves and ticklish air,
Who knew the woods could hold such flair?

So if you roam where the moonlight beams,
Don't fear the spirits, they're not what they seem.
At night, they gather for a giggle or two,
In this funny wood, there's laughter for you!

Tales Entwined in Twigs

In tangled twigs, the stories lie,
Of ants who learned to swim and fly.
A caterpillar's dream to dance and twirl,
With a thousand laughs, their tales unfurl.

One twig declares, 'I'm the tallest here!'
While another quips, 'That's just sheer cheer!'
A lizard laughs with a wink and a grin,
'In this company, we all can win!'

Old turtles boast of races past,
But everyone knows the turtles last.
They reminisce while munching leaves,
A feast of humor that truly deceives!

So listen closely to the stories they weave,
In the heart of the forest, you'll certainly believe.
That twigs have tales and giggles galore,
In this land of fun, you'll always want more!

The Silences of Sunlight and Shade

Under sunbeams, the grasshoppers jump,
While shadows hide squirrels with a thump.
A moment of stillness, then laughter breaks,
As they share their jokes with the wind and the lakes.

The sun winks down, bright as can be,
While the mushrooms whisper a secret glee.
The daisies chuckle, a floral jest,
"Why did the bee take a nap with the rest?"

The shadows stretch, with an echoing yawn,
As the fern fans flicker, dancing till dawn.
Each leaf a partner in this playful show,
Nature's humor, a grand overflow!

So find a patch where light meets the dark,
Join in the laughter, let out a spark.
In this blend of silence, find joy that's displayed,
In every laugh shared, a love never swayed!

Shadows Reveal Their Secrets

In the nook of the old oak tree,
Squirrels gossip with such glee.
They chatter loud, then quickly hide,
As if their secrets can't abide.

The sunbeams dance, their laughter bright,
Frogs leap about, what a silly sight!
They croak their tales, quite bold and brash,
While beetles roll around, they crash!

A rabbit grins, with mischief planned,
A tickle here, a playful hand.
The grasshoppers join in the fun,
In this green jest, they've surely won!

So when the shadows softly creep,
Nature's giggles wake from sleep.
Join the giggle, sing along,
In this leafy realm, we all belong!

Renewed Echoes of the Earth

Beneath the sky so wide and blue,
A dandelion, spry, bids adieu.
Its yellow crown, now flying high,
A fuzzy joke, a ball of pie!

The ants parade, a brisk brigade,
Each one's a soldier, unafraid.
To nibble crumbs, they march in line,
They're on a quest for crumbs divine!

The wind can't stop its playful game,
It tousles leaves; oh, what a shame!
Each blade of grass tells a pun,
In this giggly dance, we've just begun!

So tune your ears to earth's embrace,
With every step, a jolly chase.
Let laughter roll like a gentle stream,
In nature's pranks, we're all a team!

The Sigh of the Serene Glen

In the glen where mushrooms sway,
Toadstools frown and shout, 'Hey!'
With polka dots and silly hats,
They giggle soft, just like old bats.

The gentle brook hums a tune,
While frogs put on a hopping show,
With splashes wide, they seek the moon,
In their troupe, there's never foe!

The daisies talk, with petals white,
Each gossiping flower, what a sight!
They share their dreams in a breeze so light,
Telling tales of the starry night.

With every sigh and dreamy glance,
Life breaks into a merry dance.
Rest your heart in the jocund green,
In this serene, funny routine!

Silent Stories Carved in Wood

The trees stand tall, with minds so vast,
Each knot and swirl, a tale from the past.
Bark creaks softly, 'Do you see?'
The twig that once was a bumblebee!

A chipmunk peeks from his cozy nook,
Reading a story like an open book.
His paws are full of nutty dreams,
While branches laugh, or so it seems!

The shadows play, a jigsaw shape,
A mystery hidden, a woodland drape.
Laughter dances on every bough,
Where squirrels plot, even here and now!

So bring your chuckle, join the fun,
In this forest where stories run.
Listen close, let your heart be good,
In this curious world, our laughter's wood!

Rustle of Hidden Thoughts

In the forest, secrets play,
As squirrels joke and dance all day.
Leaves giggle soft, a rustling cheer,
While acorns try to persevere.

Breezes tease the branches high,
Frogs croak tunes, oh me, oh my!
Chipmunks chuckle with each leap,
Nature's humor runs so deep.

The wise old owl gives a wink,
He snickers loud, makes you think.
Crickets chirp in funny flocks,
Life's a joke, tickling the clocks.

Underneath the leafy dome,
Every critter calls it home.
With laughter shared, no need to grieve,
In jest, we find what we believe.

Songs of the Autumn Breeze

A gust of wind sings a tune,
Turning leaves to laugh at noon.
Pumpkins grin with silly glee,
While silly scarecrows dance with me.

Crisp apples roll, a playful race,
Down the hill, they find their place.
The chilly air has jokes to share,
Tickling tissues, up in the air!

Sunlight dances on the ground,
As laughter echoes all around.
Every rustle holds a jest,
Nature's stand-up at its best!

Underneath the fiery trees,
Chirping birds are sure to tease.
With a wink and nudge, they leave,
In autumn's grasp, we simply weave.

Subtle Currents of the Wild

In the brook, giggles arise,
Fish splash high, to our surprise.
Turtles grin, basking on logs,
While ducks quack out the latest gags.

Bees hum tunes, a buzzing band,
As butterflies twirl, a swirling strand.
Nature's comedy drapes the trees,
With laughter flowing on the breeze.

Foxes prance with a playful flair,
Chasing shadows without a care.
Whiskers twitch, and tails all curl,
In this wild, we dance and twirl.

A secret show in the sunlit glade,
As critters frolic, jokes are made.
With subtle nudges and cheery tease,
In the wild, we find such ease.

Lullabies of the Ferns

In the dusk, ferns start to chat,
Tickling toes of a resting cat.
Mossy stones listen, all aglow,
As chirping crickets join the show.

The moon peeks through with a soft sigh,
As fireflies twinkle, oh my, oh my!
Breezes hum a calming song,
While dreams and giggles weave along.

With every rustle, tales unfold,
Of silly mischief and adventures bold.
Ferns sway softly, secrets shared,
In this night, we're all prepared.

So close your eyes, let laughter ring,
As nature rocks you, sweetly sing.
In every corner of the night,
Lullabies whisper pure delight.

Lullabies of the Leafy Realm

In a forest where giggles bloom,
Squirrels debate on the best costume.
A raccoon juggles acorns with pride,
While turtles race, but one forgot to glide.

The breeze hums tunes from tall trees,
Where birds harmonize, if you just sneeze.
Frogs play chess by the lilypad lake,
And a rabbit's nap makes the owls quake.

Underneath branches they conspire,
With nutty wishes they'll never tire.
A gust takes hats off unsuspecting friends,
And laughter spreads as the nonsense blends.

In shadows where mischief can thrive,
The creatures giggle, they're very much alive.
Stars peek through in the twilight hour,
As these leafy pals unite in power.

Constellations of Dappled Light

In the canopy, light dons a disguise,
Where ladybugs plot, oh what a surprise!
Fireflies dance in stars' playful spark,
While crickets hum tunes in the dark.

A picnic hosted by ants in a line,
Sharing crumbs, oh isn't it divine?
A bumblebee buzzes with sweet complaint,
While a wise old owl sketches the quaint.

Toadstools have secrets, they giggle and quake,
As mushrooms take turns in a wild little shake.
The sunlight giggles, peeking nearby,
While squirrels pose for a photo, oh my!

In dappled light where shadows prance,
All tiny critters join in a dance.
With every rustle, stories unfold,
Of silly adventures they've joyfully told.

The Unseen Dance of the Wild

In the twilight, secrets start to spin,
A hedgehog whispers, 'Let the fun begin!'
With twirls and whirls, the grass blades sway,
As the hare hops high, in a playful display.

Beetles form conga lines in a row,
While butterflies laugh, "Look at us go!"
The dance floor's set beneath the bright moon,
As fireflies shine to a happy tune.

A fox in a hat tries to balance a pie,
While skunks do a shimmy and owls just sigh.
In the midnight hush, their giggles ignite,
With every slide, there's a fresh delight.

Each rustle and chuckle blends with the night,
As laughter cascades in the gentle twilight.
In the wild's unseen gig, every creature plays,
In the heart of the forest, under starlit rays.

Harmonies in the Hush

In the stillness, laughter holds its breath,
Where critters plot and words, they bequeath.
A mouse in sunglasses counts to ten,
While the hedgehog wonders where all the friends went.

Squirrels play tag in a leaf pile high,
As raccoons debate who can reach the sky.
With twigs for instruments, they form a band,
Under the moonlight, they take a stand.

The wind carries giggles across the ground,
As every creature joins in, joy is profound.
Branches sway gently, as if to agree,
That humor is best when shared in a spree.

In this tranquil realm where the tall trees sway,
Nature's hilarity gallops and plays.
With each rustle of foliage, fun flows free,
In the calm of the hush, it's a jubilant spree.

Conversations with the Rustling Canopy

In the branches, giggles play,
Squirrels gossip all the day.
Leaves shake hands, a playful cheer,
"Did you see that bird? It's here!"

Underneath, the rabbits dance,
Frogs croak in a crazy trance.
Chasing shadows, playing tag,
While the owls just sit and brag.

A breeze hums jokes that fly by,
Even butterflies drop a sigh.
Roots chuckle with each small breeze,
Nature's laughter heard with ease.

Twirling vines—oh, what a sight!
Mice are cartwheeling with delight.
In this grove, each tree's a friend,
With each leaf, stories never end.

The Language of Falling Leaves

Golden leaves fall with a thud,
They talk a lot, but sound like mud.
"Catch me, catch me!" they all shout,
As they flutter and swirl about.

A maple says, "I'm hottest today!"
While the oak rolls eyes, "No way!"
As pine needles laugh in a swirl,
Even branches start to twirl.

Each gust carries secrets loud,
Singing praises to the crowd.
Rusty tones are high in zest,
In this rustle, life is best.

Fallen friends pile up with glee,
Pretending they're a cozy tree.
In this chattering, giggling scene,
The forest thrives, know what I mean?

The Quietude of Nature's Heart

In the stillness, birds play tricks,
Chirping tunes like little flicks.
Growing banter, soft and light,
As crickets join the fun at night.

A hedgehog rolls, his spines a mess,
The chipmunks laugh, "What a stress!"
Nature's pause, with jests so sweet,
Where every echo feels like a treat.

Mossy stones hold quiet chats,
As squirrels chatter about their hats.
Leaves giggle, and flowers cheer,
In this calm, no need for fear.

Life slows down, yet spirits soar,
With each rustle, who could ask for more?
In this hush, find joy and art,
In the gentle pulse of nature's heart.

Soft Serenades Between the Trees

Trees hum softly, what's the news?
Fungi snicker in their shoes.
Breeze carries songs, oh so light,
Twirling leaves in pure delight.

Barking dogs join in the fun,
While acorns plot a big run.
Bouncing branches sway and wink,
As earthworms laugh, give a blink.

The shadows stretch, a tickle here,
Where whispers of fun fill the air.
A butterfly dons a funny face,
And twirls around in a merry chase.

In this glen of giggles bright,
Laughter dances, pure delight.
Nature's show, no need to rehearse,
In the forest, it's all verse!

In the Company of Elder Trees

There once stood a tree with a laugh so loud,
It tickled the branches and drew quite a crowd.
The squirrels all giggled, the rabbits did dance,
While birds held their sides, they took quite a chance.

A critter approached with a serious face,
Said, "Tree, tell us now, what's your favorite place?"
The tree chuckled back, "Why, here's where I thrive,
Enjoying the jokes that keep the woods alive!"

The Hidden Cadence of the Wilderness.

In the depths of the woods, where the shadows prance,
The raccoons have secret meetings and dance.
They wear tiny hats, oh what a sight,
Debating the best way to snag food at night.

A deer with a monocle joined in the fray,
Arguing passionately about new grass today.
When a fox chimed in with a witty remark,
"Let's stick to the plan, or we'll miss the park."

Secrets of the Canopy

Up high in the branches, the birds share a tale,
Of a squirrel who thought he could outrun a snail.
With wings all a-flutter, they burst into song,
While the snail just smiled, knowing he's strong.

A wise owl observed with a glimmering eye,
As the drama unfolded beneath the blue sky.
He hooted, "Oh dear, what a comedy show!
Just wait 'til you see how fast they can go!"

Shadows in the Swaying Foliage

In the dappled spots where the sunlight peeks,
A dance party starts, hear the branches squeak.
The beetles in tuxedos parade in a line,
While ladybugs laugh, sipping dew like fine wine.

A twig snapped loudly, the crowd held its breath,
Turns out it was just a leaf dealing death.
"Let's keep the festivities under control,
Or we'll scare off the critters who bring us our soul!"

Nature's Softened Chorus

Squirrels chatter, tales absurd,
Bugs play tag, it's all unheard.
Bees hum softly, a buzzing tune,
While frogs croak out their jumbled rune.

The trees shrug, wearing leafy hats,
Rabbits hop, like sprightly acrobats.
Sunbeams wink from above the boughs,
Nature's giggles, oh, how it allows!

A duck quacks jokes, in the pond it dips,
Fish splash back with comical flips.
Even the clouds seem to grin and play,
As nature's chorus brightens the day.

Concealed Cadences of the Woods

In the thicket, a rustle's found,
Mice plotting schemes, all around.
A deer trips over a tiny root,
Cackling at squirrels in pursuit!

A snicker from the towering oaks,
As branches tremble with whispered jokes.
The owls hoot, with a knowing cheer,
Chasing shadows, far and near.

Twigs snap loud—a clumsy dance,
Bears stumble, taking a chance.
Nature chuckles with glee and zest,
In this secret realm, all jesters rest.

Beneath the Dance of Light

Sunbeams jiggle upon the ground,
Dancing daisies make silly sounds.
A ladybug struts, full of pride,
While butterflies flutter, side to side.

A shadow passes, what could it be?
A cat? A ghost? Just a bumblebee!
With every glance, there's laughter near,
As tadpoles tumble without any fear.

Ants march on, a wiggly line,
With carrying crumbs, oh-so-fine!
The grassy stage calls for a cheer,
Amidst the giggles, nature's veneer.

Lingering Laughter of the Wild

Frogs wear crowns made of lily pads,
While raccoons practice their silly fads.
A turtle grins, taking its time,
As squirrels engage in acrobatic mime.

Crickets chirp in offbeat tune,
Creating music beneath the moon.
The wind joins in with a gentle tease,
Shaking branches like ticklish trees.

In the glade, echoes of joy bloom,
With every rustle, the wild finds room.
Nature's antics—oh, what a spree!
In this lively show, everyone's free!

Veiled Conversations in the Woods

Squirrels gossip, tails in a twist,
They plot their heists, a nutty tryst.
Mice roll their eyes at the squirrel's schemes,
While birds just chuckle, lost in their dreams.

Leaves dance with joy, telling jokes up high,
The sun winks down, he's a clever spy.
A deer steps in, but trips on a root,
Skidding away in a comic hoot!

Frogs croak laughter, ribbits in style,
Each jump's a story, they share with a smile.
Raccoons on raccoons, a trash can debate,
Who swiped the pie? They all just can't wait!

The whole wood chuckles, a giggling crowd,
Nature's own stand-up, bold and loud.
As dusk pulls the curtain on this leafy stage,
The forest erupts, a comedic page!

Tales of the Woodland Spirits

The spirits gather around the old tree,
Trading quips with a whimsical glee.
One floats in circles, a ghostly ballet,
While another juggles acorns, come what may.

Mushrooms nod, with caps like hats,
Sharing secrets of the cheeky bats.
Raccoons roll dice on the old wooden stump,
And giggles erupt with each playful jump.

A breeze tells tales of a lost pair of socks,
While hedgehogs sip tea, wearing their frocks.
Each tale's a puzzle, thick as the night,
Making the moon chuckle, glowing so bright.

Fireflies flash, a dance to impress,
Nature's own party, no need to dress.
With laughter and games till the break of dawn,
The woodland spirits will keep rolling on!

Whispers of the Wind's Embrace

The wind spins stories, oh what a delight,
Telling tales of mischief, day and night.
A gust carries giggles from tree to tree,
Even the bushes chuckle, wild and free.

A playful rabbit hops, with ears in the air,
He tickles the leaves without a care.
Acorns rumble, their comedy show,
As leaves rustle softly, joining the flow.

A fox in a scarf makes a stylish dash,
But tripping on roots, he turns it to flash.
The owls just hoot, with wisdom to share,
Teaching the young ones how not to care.

In the heart of the woods, a laughter parade,
The sun peeks in, its spotlight displayed.
With every rustle, the fun never ends,
Nature's a stage, with giggling friends.

Hidden Voices in the Green

In a patch of ferns, the chatter is loud,
With beetles reciting their poems, so proud.
Snakes tell tall tales, each one more absurd,
While chatting with bunnies, who barely heard.

A pigeon coos softly, sharing his woes,
About a lost crumb that nobody knows.
The ants march by, with a plan and a grin,
Dreaming of cookies, now where to begin?

Trees swap their secrets in rustles and sighs,
As sunlight streams down with glimmering eyes.
The whole forest chuckles in silly repose,
Surprising the deer, who's stuck with a rose.

With laughter like music, across all the glen,
Even the rocks join in with a zen.
Amidst the green wonders, hilarity thrives,
In this playful world, oh how laughter survives!

Secrets of the Forest Floor

The acorns roll, they start to race,
The squirrels have a lively chase.
With nuts in paws, they leap and bound,
Who knew the woods were this profound?

A mushroom grins, it's quite a sight,
It jokes with ferns late into night.
The roots all chuckle in their home,
While ladybugs begin to roam.

A beetle boasts of plans so grand,
A castle built from grains of sand.
But when the rain begins to pour,
He slips and lands—what a uproar!

The little critters gather round,
In nature's laughter, joy is found.
With every rustle, giggle sprouts,
In secret meetings of laughing outs.

Murmurs in the Canopy

High above, the branches sway,
A parrot gives the trees a play.
He cracks a joke, the crows all caw,
"The wind just lost a game of claw!"

The owls blink and roll their eyes,
"Who needs the sun to feel so wise?"
They hoot and holler, full of cheer,
A night club vibe with branches near.

The raccoons swing from vine to vine,
Sharing secrets, feeling fine.
"Did you hear 'bout the crow who danced?
He twirled and spun, left all entranced!"

A gust of wind brings leaves to play,
"Let's vote the funniest on display!"
The forest laughs, together gleams,
In treetop tales, they share their dreams.

Echoes Among the Branches

Bouncing acorns play peek-a-boo,
"Catch me if you can!" they coo.
A family of hedgehogs giggle,
While twigs below begin to wiggle.

Silly raccoons wear old hats,
Trying to dance, what funny brats!
They tumble down, the laughter flows,
Nature's own comical show.

The trees all sway with amused grace,
As chipmunks race, they set the pace.
"Who's got the biggest stash of food?"
Each little critter in good mood!

In echoes sweet, a ripple grows,
As laughter blooms where no one knows.
Amidst the shade and sunlight's tease,
The forest chuckles in the breeze.

Shadows of the Silent Grove

In shadows deep, the shadows chat,
A lost shoe waits for its owner—fat!
"I swear I left it by the tree!"
The fox just laughs, "It looks like me!"

The turtles ponder in slow jest,
"Love is grand, but food is best!"
As mushrooms dance a polka tune,
The shadows join, beneath the moon!

Beneath the canopy, humor hides,
As playful breezes pull the tides.
A nightingale sings in sweet refrain,
While shadows whisper, "Dance again!"

The moon itself has joined the fun,
With beams of light, the laughter's spun.
In every corner, joy's alive,
Where silent secrets jump and thrive.

The Secret Life of the Sylvan

In the branches, squirrels plot,
Mischief managed — it's what they've got.
They wear tiny hats, and shades with flair,
Laughing loudly, without a care.

Beneath the trees, the rabbits dance,
Debating who has the best chance.
With tiny bows and arrows, they aim,
At the dandelions,'s their favorite game.

A deer plays chess, and brings a snack,
While birds critique, they've got the knack.
The forest floor is a circus ground,
Where giggles echo and joys abound.

As twilight spills its golden hue,
Frogs hop in tuxedos, a formal view.
The woods are alive with laughter and jest,
In this secret life, they're truly blessed.

Soft Soliloquies of the Sylvan Realm

Amidst the ferns, a chipmunk sings,
About the latest gossip, and silly things.
A turtle shrugs, 'I move quite slow,'
While ants in a parade, put on a show.

A wise old owl with glasses on,
Claims he's the best, the king of dawn.
But the butterflies laugh, with colors bright,
While newbies stumble, in pure delight.

A raccoon wears socks, all mismatched,
Stealing snacks, he's been dispatched.
While hedgehogs play cards beneath the sun,
Looking quite serious, though it's all in fun.

And as the stars own the navy skies,
Fireflies blink, while the crickets cry.
Nature's humor, wrapped in the night,
In this soft soliloquy, all feels right.

Encrypted Echoes of Enchantment

In a whispering breeze, the trees conspire,
To share tales of gnomes who never tire.
They prank the mushrooms, paint them pink,
While rabbits giggle at what they think.

A badger in a bowtie struts with pride,
With a crooked smile, he walks wide-eyed.
He stops to check his lavender hue,
While the foxes snicker, what else is new?

An elf lays traps for a wayward sprite,
Who steals the moon's glow in the middle of night.
But instead, he finds cheese, oh what a fate,
Twinkling with laughter, they all celebrate.

A nightingale pens sonnets of cheer,
'A life in the woods is the life we revere!'
As shadows grow long, and giggles swell,
In their encrypted tales, all is well.

Murmurs from the Heart of the Woods

Under a canopy, a raccoon dines,
With gourmet acorns, and berry wines.
He giggles at squirrels who fumble their stash,
As the others gather to watch the crash.

A hedgehog so bold, wears a crown made of twigs,
Declaring himself the king of the digs.
While bees throw a party, music anew,
As they salsa dance, with a sticky crew.

A grassy knoll hosts a cabaret,
Where frogs croak tunes that lead the way.
As fireflies twinkle, creating the lights,
The woodland creatures enjoy their nights.

With laughter painted across the scene,
In this heart of the woods, life's a dream.
Murmurs of joy, a comedy grand,
In the funny forest, where all understand.

Songbirds' Secrets in Soft Hues

In branches high, they chuckle loud,
A serenade, they sing, quite proud.
Each note a giggle, each trill a joke,
As sunlight dances, and shadows poke.

With feathers bright, they play around,
Sneaky plans on playful ground.
A wormy feast, oh, what a find!
Their laughter echoes, truly unrefined.

In the trees, mischief will prevail,
They'd swap the tales that feisty snails tell.
Among the boughs, secrets take flight,
A raucous chorus from morning to night.

As dusk draws near, they share one last jest,
In this leafy realm, they're truly blessed.
With a flick of a wing, and a cheeky grin,
Their tales and tunes will always begin.

Stories of the Understory

Down below, where shadows play,
A chipmunk tells of his busy day.
With a nut in hand, he spills his tea,
Where all the squirrels sit, quite carefree.

A beetle struts in shiny black,
Claiming he found the best snack pack.
With friends around, they laugh and cheer,
While a clever frog croaks loudly, "Here!"

In this tangle of roots, tales are spun,
Of daring feats and forgotten fun.
The underbrush hums with secrets to keep,
As critters join in, no time for sleep.

So gather all, no need to rush,
As they weave their yarns in a playful hush.
Old leaves listen to stories that thrive,
In the heart of the woods, life feels alive.

Beneath the Rustle of Time

A squirrel dropped acorns with such flair,
While poise and grace, he would not share.
He flips and flops with each tiny fall,
As giggles echo through the leafy hall.

The wind whispers back in playful tones,
A dance of laughter; nature's own clones.
Each crackling leaf holds tales so bright,
Of cheeky antics beneath moonlight.

On sunny days, the shadows stretch wide,
As critters join in the joyful ride.
With time as their game, they bounce and mate,
In this woodland circus, they celebrate fate.

So listen close, oh you who roam,
For silly secrets in nature's home.
Amid the rustling, if you look kind,
You'll catch the humor that life designed.

Dreams Wrapped in Moss

In a cozy patch where the moss grows thick,
A sleepy tortoise draws quite a trick.
He dreams of racing, oh what a sight,
While snoring softly, he gives quite a fright!

The mushrooms nod as they hear him snore,
"I could outrun him, just once, maybe more!"
The shadows chuckle, the breezes weave,
In this forest realm, mischief's hard to believe.

A lazy frog croaks tales of his quest,
For the fluffiest lily, he claims to be blessed.
With bug-eyed wonder, they share his delight,
In dreams wrapped softly, all through the night.

As dawn breaks slowly, they rub their eyes,
And carry on with their playful lies.
For in this glen, with mossy embrace,
Every corner hides laughter's trace.

Under the Canopy of Dreams

In a forest where squirrels wear hats,
And raccoons dance like clever acrobats.
The owls throw parties, each night they gleam,
While the frogs all croak out a ribbiting theme.

The trees gossip sweetly, their branches sway,
As the chipmunks mischief their playful ballet.
With mushrooms in rows like a tiny parade,
Nature's own circus, a curious charade.

Breezes tickle tiptoes, a gentle tease,
While rabbits juggle carrots with such great ease.
Beneath the green sky, laughter takes flight,
In a world where each critter is ready to light.

So come take a peek, where the fun never ends,
Beneath leafy laughter, all creatures are friends.
In this jubilant jungle, no room for despair,
Just love and delight in the cool evening air.

Silhouette Songs in the Twilight

Bats strum on guitars made of silken thread,
While mice tap dance happily over their bed.
Crickets compose with a symphony's flair,
The moon sprinkles sparkles like floral confetti in the air.

Fireflies flicker like a light show gone wild,
As shadows of critters play games, so beguiled.
Hedgehogs in tuxedos come out for a spin,
While the anemones giggle at whom might win.

The hedges hum notes of long-hidden rhymes,
Twirling to rhythms of lost, ancient times.
In this dance of delight, all feelings uplift,
As owlets toss in a delightful cliff.

So sway with the silhouettes, feel prose come alive,
Where even the thorns learn to giggle and thrive.
In harmonies sweet under twilight's soft charm,
The night plays a concert, with no hint of alarm.

The Echoes of Twilight's Touch

A raccoon with a monocle scours through the night,
Taking notes on the giggles, all just out of sight.
While shadows of mushrooms engage in a race,
And a frog takes a leap with the grandest of grace.

Snapdragons chuckle at the mix-up of bees,
Trying to gather nectar while catching some breeze.
And hedges parade in a vibrant sly style,
Waving like dancers on an enchanted aisle.

The stars laugh along as they twinkle and twirl,
Creating a waltz for the night owl's whirl.
Amongst the tree roots, the whispers all seethe,
As winks from the branches play tricks up their sleeves.

So join in the merriment, let your heart sing,
In this hilarious veil, let joy be your king.
For every little creature now sways and now grins,
Under the spell where the laughter begins.

Timeless Calls of the Wilderness

In the jungle where laughter tickles the air,
A bear with a bowtie draws quite a stare.
Lemurs spin tales from their lofty high perches,
While the butterflies giggle over playful searches.

Bunny loves yoga, perfecting each pose,
While crickets are crooning, their music they chose.
Each twig holds a secret, a snicker or two,
As the glow-worms flash their bright lamps, just for you.

The bees crash the soirée, buzzing offbeat,
While the ants march along to a comical beat.
The trees twist and giggle, their branches do sway,
Echoing chuckles till the break of the day.

So come to this festival, join in the spree,
Where nature's delight is wild and carefree.
In every corner, find a world so bizarre,
With jokes from the wildlife, a laugh awaits far.

www.ingramcontent.com/pod-product-compliance
Lightning Source LLC
Chambersburg PA
CBHW071827160426
43209CB00003B/222